SCRUM

The First Agile Methodology For Managing Product Development Step-By-Step

©Copyright 2018 Harry Altman - All rights reserved.

If you would like to share this book with another person, please purchase an additional copy for each recipient. Thank you for respecting the hard work of this author. Otherwise, the transmission, duplication or reproduction of any of the following work including specific information will be considered an illegal act irrespective of whether it is done electronically or in print. This extends to creating a secondary or tertiary copy of the work or a recorded copy and is only allowed with express written consent from the publisher. All additional rights reserved.

TABLE OF CONTENTS

INTRODUCTION

Agile software development is gaining a lot of popularity due to its incremental nature, flexibility to change and its multifaceted collaborative and self-organizing teams.

This provides the perfect solution for companies such as start-ups that are not resource heavy and which need to respond to market conditions pretty quickly. Modern-day Agile owes its proliferation to the Agile Manifesto which was published in 2001 by a group of veterans who came together to discuss lightweight and flexible development methods. The rest, as they say, is history!

There are several popular Agile processes such as Extreme Programming or XP, Scrum, pair programming, acceptance testing and feature-driven development, to name a few. Perhaps the most popular and widely used today is Scrum.

Scrum was formalized in 1993 by Ken Schwaber and Dr. Jeff Sutherland. Scrum has been successfully implemented at many top organizations around the globe such as Yahoo, Capital One, GE and Thoughtworks. So what exactly is Scrum, and how is it different from the many other methodologies or frameworks out there?

The word 'scrum' is derived from the game of rugby where a team collectively moves down the field to reach its goal. Scrum is an empirical process that encourages teams to challenge themselves a little more every time. Scrum follows a process of 'Inspect' and 'Adapt'. Frequent inspection exposes issues or barriers and the team then adapts its approach as needed. This shorter feedback loop ensures that any product flaws are fixed early in the cycle.

Scrum is made up of certain roles, artifacts and time boxes. A Scrum team is made up of 5-7 people. Let us have a brief look at the various components of Scrum.

Scrum is one of the simplest "agile" methodologies and is also proven to be highly effective for both software development and more general product development. Scrum is often used in financial product development.

Scrum is based on the idea that during a project the customers will almost certainly change their minds about what they want and need. To address this, a Scrum project moves forward in a series of short iterations, each of which delivers an incremental set of improvements to the product.

Scrum has frequent intermediate deliveries with working functionality. This enables the customer to get a working product earlier and enables the project to change its requirements according to changing needs.

Scrum provides a set of practices and predefined roles which a team adopts in order to maximize the team's ability to deliver quickly and respond to changing and emerging requirements.

Scrum defines only three roles for its development team. These are the Product Owner, the ScrumMaster, and the Team. There is typically one Product Owner who serves as the customer or customer proxy and finalizes the requirements. The Scrum Master is the process owner who mainly works on removing any barriers the team faces and ensures that Scrum is followed correctly. The Team is any team member other than the Product Owner or Scrum Master. This could be a programmer, tester, business analyst, architect etc. Scrum encourages its team members to wear different hats and it is very common to find team members pitching in as and where needed.

In Scrum lingo, the team members are called pigs whereas external resources are called chickens. This stems from a story about a pig and chicken planning to open a restaurant called 'ham and eggs'. The pig would be 'committed' since its hide is on the line, while the chicken is only 'involved'.

Scrum is made up of iterations or 'sprints'. These may have any length ranging from one week to four weeks. Sprints start and end at a fixed time irrespective of whether the targeted work is finished. This aspect is called a 'time box' which will be explained below in further detail.

CHAPTER 1

WHAT IS SCRUM?

Scrum is a simple project management framework for incremental product development that has become wildly popular in the software development community.

Usually paired with engineering practices from the eXtreme Programming (XP) community, Scrum is one exponent of the agile movement and represents a paradigmatic shift from "waterfall," a traditional project management approach that, until recently, has dominated software development.

The Scrum method is deliberately designed as a framework, i.e. a lightweight management wrapper that can be applied to existing processes. However, every part of Scrum's minimal framework is essential for realizing its core tenets of facilitating productivity through communication, collaboration, and self-organization. Given its spare structure, it's critical that all of Scrum's roles and processes are observed. Here's a quick overview of Scrum's primary roles and meetings.

SCRUM ROLES

The Scrum framework includes only three roles: The Product Owner, the Scrum team, and the ScrumMaster.

1.   The Product Owner is the single individual responsible for the success of a project, which entails communicating the product vision to team members and negotiating sprint goals with them. As such, this person constantly reprioritizes the Product Backlog to reflect those items which will yield the highest business value. Because the Product Owner is responsible for generating a return on investment, this role possesses the authority to accept or reject each product increment at the sprint review meeting, which occurs at the conclusion of each sprint.

2.   The Scrum team is a cross-functional and self-organizing team of about seven members (plus or minus two) that is responsible for delivering a functional product increment each sprint. During the Sprint Planning meeting, the team negotiates the work it will tackle each sprint with the Product Owner and then, during the sprint, determines amongst its members how to complete that work.

3.   The ScrumMaster facilitates team productivity and self-organization by removing impediments that obstruct progress, reminding all team members to observe Scrum's rules, and ensuring that all Scrum artifacts remain highly visible. It is important to note that the ScrumMaster has no

authority. This role functions as a servant-leader. Therefore, it is recommended that individuals who derive satisfaction from a team's success, not just individual heroics, are best suited for this position.

SCRUM MEETINGS

The Scrum framework includes four main meetings (Sprint Planning, the Daily Standup, Sprint Reviews, and the Sprint Retrospectives) as well as one important ancillary meeting, Backlog Grooming.

1.   During the Sprint Planning meeting, the Product Owner and the team negotiate the work that team members will attempt to complete in the next sprint. The product owner is responsible for identifying the highest priority work, while the team is responsible for committing to the amount of work it can accomplish within the confines of the sprint.

2.   The Daily Standup meeting allows team members to deliver updates and exchange information on a daily basis. Every day, at the same time and place, team members spend fifteen minutes reporting to one another. Each team member reports to the rest of the team what they did since the previous meeting, what will be done before the next one, and what impediments obstruct progress.

3.   The Sprint Review meeting occurs at the end of each sprint. At this meeting, the team demonstrates the functional product increment it has developed and the Product Owner either accepts or rejects the work, based on the previously negotiated agreement. This is an opportunity to "inspect and adapt" - that is, to examine the product's progress and revise direction, if necessary, for future sprints.

4.   The Sprint Retrospective provides the team with an occasion to inspect and adapt its own processes. During this meeting, the team reflects on its performance in the past sprint and brainstorms ways to improve going forward.

5.   Backlog Grooming, which is known as the fifth Scrum meeting, creates a dedicated time for the Product Owner and team to come together to prepare the backlog prior to the Sprint Planning meeting. Scrum literature recommends that teams spend five percent of their sprint on backlog grooming.

Although Scrum is a relatively skeletal framework, it is essential that practitioners acknowledge how purposeful its construction is. Each role of the framework is designed to create balance in terms of both authority and responsibility for the members of a Scrum team, while Scrum's few meetings and artifacts sketch out necessary milestones within the development cycle. Of course, there are ways in which organizations can modify the framework to suit particular needs, but these basic aspects should remain intact and provide users with a roadmap for effective, continually improving product development and delivery.

SCRUM ARTIFACTS

The main artifacts that are produced in Scrum are the Product Backlog, Sprint Backlog, Sprint Burndown and Release Burndown.

The Product Backlog is an ordered list of all the features that the customer might want in the product. The highest priority features are at the top ensuring that the most important and highest value functionality is built first. The Sprint Backlog has a limited scope. It consists of features from the Product Backlog that are going to be built in that particular sprint. Any work that is not done at the end of the sprint goes back to the product backlog for reprioritization.

The Sprint Burndown chart tells us how much time is left before we reach our goal. It tracks the work done every day and is relevant only for the given sprint. The Release Burndown chart tracks the time left up to the end of the release. It also portrays how much work is done with respect to release goals.

SCRUM TIMEBOXES

Scrum introduces the concept of a time box. This means that a given event will have a fixed time and will expire at the end of the time limit. The various meetings in Scrum are allocated a time box. The Scrum time boxes include the Sprint planning meeting, Release planning meeting, the Daily Scrum, Sprint review, and retrospectives. The Daily Scrum or stand up is always 15 minutes. The other planning meetings also have a fixed time depending on the Sprint length that the team decides on.

SCRUM ACCEPTANCE CRITERIA

Scrum introduces the concept of 'done'. This is also called success criteria or acceptance criteria and outlines the conditions a particular feature must meet in order to be considered 'done' or complete.

SCRUM STORY BOARDS AND COLLOCATION

The story board - used to portray the Sprint Backlog - is another mainstay of the Scrum process. This is a physical board in the team which could be part of a wall or several walls as required. There is a concept of a 'story' which is a feature or high-level requirement. Typically, any item from the product backlog could become one of many stories. The story states what the user accepts from a given feature. For example, 'As a user, I should be able to log in to my email'. The success criteria outline the things that must happen to consider this 'done'. All the tasks needed to plan, design, and code and test this story are placed under this. These tasks could be done by several people on the team.

Scrum encourages collocating all the team members in an open group area minus walls. The idea is to encourage open communication and reduce overheads from emails or phone calls. Impromptu discussions between the customer and team members are pretty common in a Scrum room.

INFORMATION RADIATORS

The Scrum artifacts are displayed throughout the area where the team sits and works. These include story boards, backlogs, burndown charts, barrier section, architecture maps, designs etc. The idea is that any relevant information should be easily visible to the team all the time. This is informative as well as motivational. The information radiates or jumps out from all the charts and boards. Color coding is used to differentiate tasks, stories, barriers etc. A lot of software tools are available for tracking Scrum projects, but it cannot replace the effect physical information radiators have in my opinion.

SPRINT RETROSPECTIVE

The retrospective deserves special mention. This is where the team comes together at the end of a sprint and openly talks about what went well and what could be done better. A retrospective is not to be used for finger pointing. Retrospectives become more effective as the team gels and team members trust each other and the management. This is necessary to uncover impediments that people may be hesitant to speak about in a typical controlling management structure.

SCRUM IN THE GLOBAL SCENARIO

Even though Scrum encourages collocation, it may not always be possible, especially in the case of distributed teams that are in multiple geographic locations. Scrum has been proven to be effective even in such situations and many teams practice distributed Scrum.

THE SCRUM TEAM

A Scrum team is typically cross-functional and generally consists of around 5-9 people, however, it can be much larger. The team has the responsibility to deliver the product. Scrum encourages co-location of all team members and verbal communication between team members. A number of specific roles are defined in Scrum:

THE SCRUM MASTER

Scrum projects are run using very flexible management style and require project managers with specific experience managing Agile projects. The project management role is non-traditional in that the ScrumMaster is primarily a facilitator who enforces the agreed rules, removes impediments to progress and ensures the team remains focused.

Scrum teams are self-organizing. The ScrumMaster is not the leader of the team and instead acts as a buffer between the team and any distracting influences.

PRODUCT OWNER

The Product Owner represents the customer and ensures that the Scrum Team works on the "right things" from a business perspective. The Product Owner writes customer-centric "stories" which are one or two sentences in business language describing a specific product feature. These are then implemented by the Scrum team.

STAKEHOLDERS

These are the people for whom the project will produce the agreed-upon benefits. They are only directly involved in the process during reviews of progress.

CHAPTER 2

SCRUM OF SCRUMS

The scrum framework brings structure and order to a project in a chaotic, fast-paced environment. It delivers a shippable increment of the product after each sprint and allows a business to increase return on investment through prioritization.

As long as the rules are carried out as its creators intended, the results are phenomenal and business value is realized. However, what happens when the business requires greater output, many related projects to be synchronized to a deadline or a coordinate technical solution? This is where the technique comes into its own.

The Scrum of scrums is a method of co-coordinating teams and is used to grow and synchronize the scrum framework within a company to huge scale. Scrum masters used this technique to great effect in order to keep complex inter-related projects in sync.

1.   THE CHALLENGE - SCALING

The challenge in scaling across an organization lies within the rule that a team should typically have between five and nine members. While this is a guideline and there is no substitute for common sense, teams should definitely be "lean, mean, productive machines". The challenge gets interesting when the business stakeholders wake up one morning and say, "I want to deliver quicker, let's put another thirty people on the project." Or if they say, "We need this delivered in three months and there are three other dependent teams you need to deliver this with." Breaking the news that you want to limit the team to nine members would seem to limit the ability of the business to deliver.

This technique helps in these very situations, but before I explain how it works it is important to understand that it relies on all the original rules of scrum being carried out correctly, especially product backlog management and prioritization. For this reason, the product owner's role is key to the whole process and this should be discussed with the product owner(s) and stakeholders involved before embarking on a mission in your organization.

Continue reading and you will see why this is so important.

WHAT IS SCRUM OF SCRUMS?

This is a meeting held to coordinate a set of inter-related Scrum teams. The power and ability to scale is in the fact that one representative from each related team attends the meeting. By doing this an organization can coordinate hundreds of people on different teams.

From each team, a representative has been picked to attend the meeting. The representatives share knowledge. Once the number of members in the Scrum of scrums becomes too large a representative from that meeting can join another meeting and the process can continue.

In this meeting, the host asks four questions (in the same vein as the daily scrum meeting). The questions are:

1.   What have you accomplished since the last meeting?

2.   What do you aim to accomplish before the next meeting?

3.   Are there any impediments/blockers in your way?

4.   Are you about to do anything that could create a blocker/impediment to the project?

The first three questions aim to highlight progress, draw attention to targets and surface any issues that need to be addressed to keep the project on track. The last question stems from the fact that related projects can often unknowingly create problems for each other. For example, in the technology world, one team may deploy code that means vastly more testing for another team.

The meetings can be scheduled to be as frequent as needed and are usually anywhere from daily to bi-weekly. It purely depends on the needs of the program.

SCRUM STANDUP

The heart of the Scrum process is embodied in the daily standup meeting, also commonly known as the daily Scrum, which emphasizes Scrum's tenets of communication and transparency. This meeting is critical to ensuring that every member of a development team is on the same page. Each day, a Scrum team gathers in a predetermined spot-a team room or office-to update one another on the progress made since the last meeting, what they will attempt to do before the next one, and any impediments standing in their way. These updates are commonly phrased as responses to the following three questions:

- What have I done since the last Scrum meeting (yesterday)?

- What will I do before the next Scrum meeting (tomorrow)?

- What prevents me from performing my work as efficiently as possible?

This meeting is usually time-boxed to 15 minutes. If team members need to discuss an issue that will require more time, it is recommended that the relevant individuals involved meet in a "sidebar" meeting immediately after. This way, team members only attend meetings that directly involve their work, while others can get back to work. Unfortunately, there is a tendency for daily Scrums to last longer than 15 minutes. To compensate, many teams use stopwatches or timers to uphold the time limitations. To cut down on extraneous small talk, some teams also employ a talking stick or mascot, in which the team member holding the stick or mascot is the only one permitted to talk. When they finish their update, the talking stick or mascot is passed to the next team member, who reports, and so on.

When the daily Scrum meeting occurs is something for the team and Product Owner to determine, but, most Scrum literature advocates holding the meeting early on in the day - usually as soon as all the team members arrive in the morning.

HOW TO MINIMIZE RISKS THROUGH SCRUM?

Being an Agile, iterative process, the Scrum framework inherently minimizes risk. The following Scrum practices facilitate the effective management of risk:

1.   Flexibility reduces business-environment-related risk

The risk is largely minimized in Scrum due to the flexibility in adding or modifying requirements at any time in the project lifecycle. This enables the organization to respond to threats or opportunities from the business environment and unforeseen requirements whenever they arise, with the usually low cost of managing such risks.

2.   Regular feedback reduces expectations-related risk

Being iterative, the Scrum framework gives ample opportunities to obtain feedback and set expectations throughout the project lifecycle. This ensures that the project stakeholders, as well as the team, are not caught off guard by miscommunicated requirements.

3.   Team ownership reduces estimation risk

The Scrum Team estimates and takes ownership of the Sprint Backlog Items, which leads to more accurate estimation and timely delivery of product increments.

4.   Transparency reduces non-detection risk

The Scrum principle of transparency around which the framework is built ensures that risks are detected and communicated early, leading to better risk handling and mitigation. Moreover, when conducting Scrum of Scrums Meetings, Impediments that one team is currently facing may be deemed a risk for other Scrum Teams in the future. This should be recognized in the Updated Impediments Log.

5.   Iterative delivery reduces investment risk

Continuous delivery of value throughout the Scrum project lifecycle, as potentially shippable Deliverables are created after every Sprint, reduces investment risk for the customer.

Let me explain by giving a few reasons for why Scrum always works:

1.   Communication shouldn't be the barrier

Communication among the members of the team and the clients is what gets appreciated and promoted by Scrum, which results in an attitude good for the team.

2.   Amazingly fast results

Getting the results after every few steps is what needed to get the feedback from the client, which works well and is helpful to work efficiently on the project.

3.   Stay focused

Time waste is just not the focus in this methodology as everything gets prioritized based on the importance of the item.

4.   Estimates the reasonable time

Production team's involvement makes it easier and fair to estimate the accurate time needed.

5.   Organized on own

One of the jobs of the production team is to make sure to achieve the specified goal in the desired time. A combination of skill sets and skill levels are often best to promote a continuous workflow.

6.   Open

Scrum is always transparent: From the beginning, the client knows what they can expect at the end of each step as they are the hand behind the product backlog. Within the team they also maintain equal transparency; in fact, they main it throughout the project.

Above are the reasons why Scrum always works for us.

CHAPTER 3

SCRUM SOFTWARE DEVELOPMENT METHODOLOGY

Implementation of Agile (Scrum) Software Development Methodology

The implementation process of Scrum's methodology can easily be explained with the help of the Scrum Framework. The framework is divided into three parts, i.e. Roles, Ceremonies, and Artifacts.

ROLES

Three defined roles are a part of the Scrum methodology. These are Product Owner, The Scrum Master, and The Team Ceremonies, which are the processes involved in the implementation of the Agile (Scrum) software development methodology and include the following:

SPRINT PLANNING

The sprint planning meeting consists of team, the Scrum master, and the product owner. In the meeting, the product backlog items are discussed so that they can be prioritized and then the team selects which ones to do. The sprint planning meeting determines what will be worked on and it also helps to develop a considerable understanding of what needs to do in order carry it out. One notable thing done in sprint planning is that tasks are measured in time (whereas before it was done in story points).

A rule of thumb, a sprint planning takes approximately number of weeks in sprint * 2 hours (4 hours in our case).

DAILY SCRUM

The daily Scrum meeting is held daily for about 15 minutes. This is not a problem-solving meeting. The daily Scrum helps avoid unnecessary meetings. In the daily Scrum everyone answers three questions, which are:

- What did you do yesterday?

- What will you do today?

- Is anything in your way?

THE SPRINT REVIEW

In the Sprint Review (can also be referred to a Review & Demo) the team presents what has been accomplished during the sprint. It is a demonstration of new features or the existing architecture. It is an informal presentation and the entire team participates in it.

SPRINT RETROSPECTIVE

It involves looking at what is working and what is not. The time period for the sprint retrospective is around thirty minutes and is done after every sprint. It involves the participation of the product owner, Scrum master, team and even the customers. In the retrospective, the whole team gathers to discuss what they want to start, continue or stop doing.

ARTIFACTS

The artifacts can be called the tools of the Scrum methodology and include the following:

PRODUCT BACKLOG

The product backlog captures the requirements listed as items or works on the project. Each item is expressed in a way which provides value to the customer, prioritized by the product owner and reprioritized at the start of each sprint.

SPRINT BACKLOG

The sprint goal is a short statement about the focus of the work during the sprint. In the sprint, backlog work is never assigned and individuals choose their own work; the remaining work is estimated daily, and any member can add, changes or deletes the sprint backlog. Spring backlog determines the work for the sprint, is updated every day and each item has its own status.

SPRINT BURNDOWN CHART

The Sprint burndown chart shows the total Sprint Backlog hours remaining each day and also the estimated amount of time to release. The Sprint burndown chart should ideally come down to zero at the end of the sprint. The X-axis of the chart shows the time left in this sprint and the Y-axis show the hour's estimated remaining.

BENEFITS OF SCRUM

- Scrum methodology eliminates the need for comprehensive documentation

- Mistakes can be easily rectified

- Clear visibility of the project development

- Iterative in nature and requires customer feedback

- Short sprints and constant feedback make coping with changes easier

- Individual productivity improves as a result of daily meetings

- Issues are identified in advance and hence can be resolved rapidly

- A quality product can be easily delivered in the scheduled time

- Minimal overhead cost in terms of process and management

- It helps with the delivery of top-value features first

- Shorter time to market, which increases market feedback and ROI

- System is better prepared for adaptation to business and external changes

PITFALLS

- Tasks can be spread over several sprints if it is not well defined

- Success and failure of the projects depends on the commitment of the team members

- Heavily relies on a dedicated Product Owner. The lack of it cascades down and hinders the quality of the backlog, which has an impact on essentially the entire process

- Works well only with a small team

- Needs relatively experienced members

- Works well for project management only when the Scrum Masters trust the team

IMPLEMENTATION EXAMPLE

- A fixed time meeting is held at a fixed place each day

32

- The team Lead (Scrum Master) asks the team members about what they did previous day, what they plan to do and if any issues were observed by them

- Every day the team lead sends the report showing the daily progress and issues called a burndown chart

- A meeting is held at the beginning of the sprint by the team lead to discuss the product backlog in order to prioritize the work, resource allocation and the issues known as the sprint backlog. They meet once every week for 2 to 4 weeks

- The Product Owner defines the scope of the sprint based on the time estimates set at the sprint planning and the team's capacity for the next sprint. This scope needs to be clearly communicated to the team since completing these tickets will be a commitment for the sprint

- A daily Scrum meeting is held in order to synchronize the activities while the teams work through the spring backlog tasks

- One or more times during the sprint, a backlog grooming sessions are held to present and discuss upcoming user stories for next sprints. The output may be an estimation of a story in story points, or if the team needs more clarifications, questions that the product owner needs to research on a sprint review is conducted at the end of the sprint cycle and the finalized product is released

- Performance and improvements based on previous sprint cycle is discussed before starting with a new sprint; this is called sprint retrospective

- The sprint cycle continues

VIRTUAL SCRUM

WHAT IS VIRTUAL SCRUM?

A virtual scrum is an education tool used to help teach the scrum methodology to undergraduate students in the field of software engineering. Because this has become such a widely-used agile practice in the software industry, it's important that students get a feel for this experience in a hands-on manner. The ISISTAN-CONICET Research

Institute located in Buenos Aires, Argentina, has developed a virtual scrum program and conducted a case study to evaluate its effectiveness.

This study provided an educational and hands-on approach to scrum methodology. This virtual training tool allowed students to familiarize themselves with programs and elements of Scrum like blackboards, web browsers, document viewers, charts, and calendars.

This study followed 45 students using this program to complete their capstone project, as well as those not following the virtual scrum methodology. The results of the study confirmed that virtual tool is an excellent and efficient way to teach students the fundamentals and navigation of the Scrum methodology.

AGILE SOFTWARE DEVELOPMENT AND THE SCRUM METHODOLOGY

Annual surveys have found that agile methods like scrum have been increasing every year. The 2007 State of Agile Development Survey found that 37 percent of respondents use Scrum. And today more than 50 percent of surveyed companies have adopted Scrum as their main agile methodology. This methodology is a dependable, collective approach to software development that can be implemented in any office. This also leverages communication and team work to successfully manage product development.

So while this study has established the importance of a virtual scrum, it is important to understand how the virtual Scrum can be applied in your individual or workplace life. This study was established to help users understand the framework and capabilities involved in the scrum methodology. The virtual scrum allows users to get a 3D experience inside the world of scrum development.

This program helps users become involved in the scrum process by taking members through an incremental life cycle or sprints. These users are also able to become avatars with specific roles including Product Owner, Scrum Master, and Scrum team.

It's important to familiarize oneself with the basics of this methodology before experiencing the virtual scrum world.

This secondary tool, used to help people understand the process and actions involved during the scrum methodology, helps illustrate first-hand the benefits of this methodology. While reading and writing about the scrum methodology is a good way to learn, it's especially helpful to get real exposure to the scrum process.

The virtual Scrum not only allows users to take on important roles inside the Scrum process, but it also helps people experience other aspects of scrum development including organizing and creating user stories, planning the sprint backlog, monitoring sprint work and finishing the sprint.

All of these key steps to the process can be understood through the virtual scrum. This teaching tool is extremely valuable to the software engineering world and many great companies are searching for engineers well-versed in this area.

For those looking to get a better understanding of scrum and its processes, using the virtual Scrum program is an excellent option. The simulated scrum environment may be the next major trend in scrum education.

CHAPTER 4

WHAT IS SCRUM MASTER?

The Scrum Master's purpose is to understand the scrum rules and practices, remove any impediments or blockers to the team delivering and to help the team to understand how to self-organize and work in a Scrum manner.

The Scrum Master facilitates for the scrum team wherever it makes sense to do so. The Scrum Master is your go-to guy in terms of how the scrum framework should operate, and this applies to anyone in the organization.

The Scrum Master usually understands how to aid the product owner in maximizing return on investment from the business and helps the team to work together to be as productive as humanly possible and deliver a shippable increment of the product.

A Scrum Master should understand the rules of the scrum to an expert level. This means that anyone in the organization and any stakeholder should be able to rely on the Scrum Master for advice on the framework. It requires the ability to coach, mentor and build relationships with people at all levels of business. The role often requires a great deal of confidence and strength. This is because others may not share the experiences or beliefs of the Scrum Master and therefore they must often be convinced that Scrum's practices will solve their issues.

This is why influence, persuasion and leading by example are such important traits for scrum masters. A Scrum Master is a coach to the scrum team, and therefore strong interpersonal skills are necessary. The team should feel comfortable explaining any issues and the scrum master should be happy to help even on the busiest of days.

The relationship with the product owner is just as important as the relationship with the team. The ability to understand how to assist, motivate and coach the product owner can turn projects around. For this reason, one will need to understand the personal characteristics of the product owner as well as what scrum requires of him.

A traditional project manager often performs the role of scrum master. This can have both pros and cons. In this role, we manage the framework without managing the people. However, traditional project managers may be from the "command and control" background, which is averse to the belief in "self-organizing teams".

Prior technical or product domain experience is a strong plus since there are often situations that require you to empathize with the team and help them to solve problems. For example, experience in solving common problems such as setting up databases, breaking down large problems into small ones or just plain keeping solutions simple in the first place. This experience also helps the team, since the person in this role can often explain technical issues to the product owner and stakeholders without involving the team, hence leaving them to get on with the work.

HOW TO BE AN EFFECTIVE SCRUM MASTER?

A Scrum master plays a crucial role in the implementation of Scrum on software development projects. A Scrum Master is like a leg in the tripod of the Scrum team, with the other two being the product owner and the development team. The relationship of the product owner with the business representative is balanced out by the Scrum Master's relationship with the development team. His role is to support the team in becoming self-organized, to remove any obstacles the team might be facing and to ensure that the Scrum methodology is being followed. However, unlike the product owner, he not plays a management or supervisory role for the team.

The first step to being an effective Scrum Master is to understand the principles of Scrum extremely well. As a part of this, he should be well aware of what Scrum can and cannot achieve. He must ensure that daily Scrum meetings are held and other important processes of Scrum are followed and that the team does not veer off course.

It is important that a Scrum Master knows how to use different tools and techniques such as tracking and value of metrics, and should have knowledge of software development process and other agile methodologies. What is even more important to become an effective Scrum Master is to hone soft skills such as leadership and determination.

Adopting Scrum, especially when the team is not exposed to Scrum, can be challenging, and the change can sometimes be met with resistance. They will have to work with a lot of perseverance to overcome this and help create an atmosphere in which team members will stand behind Scrum.

They can assist the team in addressing any issues or removing any hurdles that may stand in the team's way. Possible issues could range from personality conflict to product ownership. They should facilitate the team, allowing it to self-organize and to determine the best way to deliver high value without compromising the ever-important Scrum methodology.

An effective Scrum master will strive to establish an amicable relationship between the product owner and team members. A product owner might at times be controlling and demanding. It is the Scrum Master's responsibility to be the pacifier and help the team maintain its morale and communicate effectively with the Product Owner to resolve any issues.

An important aspect of agile is that it places "individuals and interactions over processes and tools." An effective Scrum Master acts as a servant-leader. When managing the team, they do not direct the team but lead by example and also serves it by removing any impediments and allowing it to decide the best way to grow and perform. Being a servant-leader also means that theyre-communicates the project vision to ensure the team is heading in the right direction.

As a leader, it is also their responsibility to encourage the team by offerings rewards to keep the team motivated to continuously improve.

ROLE OF A SCRUM MASTER

In the Scrum method of agile software development, there are three fundamental roles: the Product Owner, the Scrum Master, and the team. The Product Owner is responsible for the success of a project. Now let's examine the Scrum Master role, who, in short, acts as a liaison, or facilitator, between the Product Owner and the development team. They are not a manager or taskmaster, never commits to working on behalf of the team, and has no actual authority over either the Product Owner of the Scrum team.

In agile software development, the Scrum Master role is a demanding part to play and requires a particular personality to do so effectively. Typically, the best Scrum Masters must be true team players, who find the accomplishments of others as gratifying as their own and can comfortably relinquish control to the Product Owner and team. As such, traditional project managers seldom make successful Scrum Masters because Scrum demands that they resist the temptation to micro-manage the development team.

So what does a Scrum Master's work with an agile software development team look like? The primary function is to remove any barriers (or "impediments") that stand in the way of sprint goals. Put another way, the Scrum Master does everything within their power to facilitate productivity. If a developer's computer breaks, it's the job of the Scrum Master to fix it or replace it. If a team room is too hot, it's the Scrum Master's task to cool it down and create a comfortable environment where developers remain focused on their work. It's easy, to sum up, the work a Scrum Master does in a sentence, but that hardly accounts for the infinite number of scenarios they might encounter while serving a development team.

But a Scrum Master's work isn't just limited to the team; they also have a responsibility to help the Product Owner maximize productivity. This might include helping to maintain the backlog and release plan or it might entail radiating Scrum artifacts - such as burndown charts - to ensure the Product Owner is apprised of the team's successes.

Using Scrum to manage agile software development is the leading strategy to help teams reduce risk and associated costs while increasing the quality of a team's releases. Through an emphasis on communication and collaboration, Scrum brings everyone together - from developers to stakeholders - to build a better product.

Following are some of the traits that I feel are essential to be a successful Scrum Master:

1.   Open minded and adaptable: Needs to think on his feet, be open to any and all suggestions and needs to adapt to dynamic project situations, possibly even suggesting alternate courses of action.

2.   Fearless Communicator: Needs to openly communicate at all times to all levels of an organizational

hierarchy; may have to be the bearer of bad news, and may have to suggest tough options. They should be strong enough to take any flak from the top management.

3.   Servant Leader: Should be devoted to the team and work tirelessly to remove the slightest impediment the team faces. A 'command and control' attitude will not do. It is important to be just a facilitator who empowers the team to do their best and lets them organize themselves.

4.   Process owner and educator: As the process owner for Scrum, they should have in-depth knowledge of the Scrum process and should be willing to disseminate this knowledge as and when needed. The Scrum Master is an educator at heart who never tires of teaching people about Scrum and acts as an evangelist.

It is also necessary (but not sufficient) that the person assuming this role should be certified by a global organization such as the Scrum Alliance. Maintaining various artifacts such as the release and sprint backlogs, burndown charts etc. is also a crucial part of this job description.

An organization that is newly embracing Agile may offer a lot of opposition to anyone performing this role. Taking any resistance in stride is just part of a typical workday for a Scrum Master.

WAYS SCRUM MASTER IMPROVES A SOFTWARE DEVELOPMENT TEAM'S PERFORMANCE

There are several ways in which the scrum master is able to improve overall performance while maintaining the structure.

1.   Strengthens agility: Scrum teams need to be able to shape-shift and go with the project flow. The agile development came about in part as a response to deficiencies in the waterfall method. Software development with Scrum focuses on the collaboration and organization of the entire team. As the leader of the team, the Scrum Master is tasked with helping the team work together while allowing for flexibility. Becoming agile and adaptable only improves the team's ability to work with all of the issues that may arise over the course of a typical project.

2.   Increases velocity: As a Scrum Master, it is your job to keep the software development team moving forward even with setbacks. Scrum masters work hard to encourage and support team members in their effort to deliver high-quality results as efficiently as possible. This involves careful documentation, managing stakeholder expectations, providing realistic time estimates, and much more.

3.   Improves communication: A Scrum team is known for its collaborative approach to software development.

Communication is at the heart of this collaboration. Daily Scrum meetings are a great way to improve the team's success. This meeting is typically brief but also extremely informative and helpful. Ongoing communication throughout the project is a trait all effective Scrum Masters share.

4.   Builds up morale: A Scrum Master has a very important perspective on the team, focusing more globally on all the people involved in the project. Working together in a close-knit style, it's necessary for the team to not only get along but to ideally develop trust and friendships. Creating an open environment where people feel valued is extremely important for the team. Even when things are going smoothly, it's important to continually strive to improve morale, encouraging team members to support one another and to effectively work through conflict, if it arises.

While a Scrum Master may not be directly involved in coding software, user experience design, or QA testing, their role on an agile team is extremely important. Not only do they tend to understand the more granular day-to-day work expectations, but they also have the bigger aerial view of the project and all of the people involved.

While the Scrum Master may be the main leader of the team, other team members are encouraged to take responsibility and initiative for their work. Many have found that this collaborative and organized approach to software development offers the best in terms of leadership and project management.

SCRUM MASTERS PRIMARY RESPONSIBILITY

Scrum Masters primary responsibility includes

1.   Isolating the team from outside distractions.

2.   Facilitating the team during daily stand ups and also in achieving consensus.

3.   Eliminating impediments both internal and external affecting a team's progress.

4.   Working with the team in setting up goals and also working towards achieving them.

5.   Maintain a balance between the team and key stakeholders of the project.

6.   Facilitate meetings.

7.   Works with the product owner in maintaining the product backlog.

8.   Protects the team from external stakeholders and internally also ensures that the team is not complacent.

48

9.   He also works with the technical team to implement technical practices required at the end of each sprint.

10.   He ensures that the team members are accountable for the commitments they make.

11.   Building the Release plan.

12.   Building the Scrum/Iteration plan.

SCRUM MASTERS CHECKLIST INCLUDES THE FOLLOWING

1.   How is my product owner doing?

2.   How is my team doing?

3.   How are our engineering practices doing?

4.   How is the organization doing?

A classic example to illustrate the role of a Scrum Master is that of a personal trainer in a gym. The personal trainer works in conjunction with the client in setting up goals, motivating and guiding him in achieving those goals. The Scrum Master has an authority given to them by the team which he can exercised in case something goes wrong. Since the Scrum Master has limited authority their role is more difficult than that of a project manager.

CHAPTER 5

RELEVANCE OF EMBRACING SCRUM

Realizing the undeniable advantages of adopting Scrum

The three reasons below justify why a project should be moved to Scrum:

Incremental, uninterrupted delivery at the conclusion of the project

Only after the completion of overall planning, analysis and designing of a project does the delivery happen with a Waterfall model. At the culmination of every 2 weeks does the delivery happen in minor portions which enables all stakeholders and the project board(s) concerned in a Scrum project to realize the achievements.

HEIGHTENED CLEARNESS AND TRANSPARENCY

Scrum involves having a clear vision as to the list related to product delivery as well as the delivery order, after which execution of work, forthright commitment declaration towards that list before the end of that 2-week duration must be carried out. A board is required to envision the work they are focused on whereby valuable lessons are imbibed from mistakes.

IMPROVED CONTROL

A strong discipline is required of the team members executing a Scrum project as Product Owners have the liberty to alter their perception (acceptance benchmarks which the team needs to adhere to) about the delivery order of products for every 2-week interval at the commencement of every single sprint.

ACCEPTING THE NECESSARY ROLE AND IMPORTANCE OF A SCRUM MASTER

Lack of discipline in adhering to the standards laid down by the Product Owners will always result in the team not achieving the benefits of Scrum for which an experienced Scrum Master is required of, who can help the team in transitioning the project towards Scrum, educating the team about Scrum rules, shaping the team towards better usage of Scrum, making stakeholders understand the value of their support towards the project and monitoring the team's work, and checking to ensure team members do not do a U-turn towards past ineffective habits.

CONDUCTING A SCRUM TRAINING INVOLVING ALL NECESSARY STAKEHOLDERS

All stakeholders including the team should be made aware of the processes, roles, control mechanisms and basic rules of Scrum so that when everyone starts working on a Scrum project, they can coordinate and work using a common language (which can happen by working right through real-time projects using Scrum). It can be done through relevant documentations available, case studies, anecdotes etc.

TRANSITIONING TO A SCRUM-ORIENTED GOVERNANCE STANDARD RELATED WITH THE DAILY PROJECT EXECUTION

Integration of PRINCE2 with Scrum can do wonders for a project as role clarification and realization of improved mitigation of risk and tolerances of projects can be achieved much more in a simplified manner. However, to satisfy Project Boards regarding reports, the team(s) can make use of statistics in terms of the level of commitment by the team and the delivery with the expected set estimates etc. in the line of Project controls set by PRINCE2.

ALLOCATING PHYSICAL SPACE FOR THE TEAM(S) INVOLVED WITH THE SCRUM PROJECT

It's vital to get authorization (if it was not there initially) for making use of some amount of physical space for the team as the team will need to - make use of whiteboards, and put up sticky notes regarding WIP or work-in-progress communication.

CREATING THE PRODUCT BACKLOG

The product backlog helps in comparing the requirements of stakeholders with the outcomes of the project through delving into the list of products, and obtaining feedback from users regarding their expectations of what and when regarding delivery will play a significant role in communication transparency.

SCRUM ROOTS AND PITFALLS TO AVOID AT ALL COSTS

Scrum, having its roots in Agile methodology, can be effectively employed for almost any type of project. However, scrum is most preferred for software development purposes. The scrum process is ideally suited for rapidly changing project environments. It is most useful, and its potential can be tapped in the best manner, when the user related requirements are changed frequently, or randomly, due to various reasons. The methodology makes it possible to incorporate the changes easily and effectively within its development cycle, and still generate positive outputs.

THE TRUE ESSENCE AND WORKING OF SCRUM

According to Scrum methodology, development occurs in short bursts of activity known as "sprints". Each sprint can generally last from two to four weeks. Each sprint begins with a meeting, known as a "sprint meeting", and typically concludes with clearly defined and set out development objectives. Sprint meetings are very brief and occur daily before the commencement of the sprint for that particular day. The main objective of the meeting is to apprise everyone about how much development progress has been made since the previous day, and what objectives are to be achieved on the particular working day. The main purpose of Scrum is to aid the team members in inspecting and adapting to the changes and providing transparency with regards the working of the project. Another main advantage offered by the Scrum framework is to increase the involvement and the interaction of the client with the team members. The client remains apprised of the most recent development status, which helps them to undertake informed decisions about what further development activities are required to complete the project in totality, and what features and functionalities need to be omitted, or which have become redundant during the development cycle.

PITFALLS WHILE IMPLEMENTING SCRUM

Scrum is a framework, a methodology based upon an organized thought process developed specially to cater to changing development requirements, and the main issue with Agile and scrum is that the methodology is to be implemented, or its rules enforced in a proper manner. Many times, when organizations are not properly trained in the implementation of the methodology, there is a tendency to fall back upon old development methods, consciously or unconsciously, thus making Scrum redundant. Traditional development methods such as Waterfall have been in existence for a long time, and people are more familiar with them. Project managers have practiced these methods for a long time, and they are more conversant with them. Scrum can be difficult to implement, and if the manager is not properly trained, they may substitute some of the scrum related processes with Waterfall methods. The objective is to provide a specific solution during the development cycle, and when the person fails to implement Scrum in a particular development related process, they "patch" up the Scrum implementation process with a Waterfall technique. This should be avoided at all costs. Scrum should be implemented in totality for it to be effective.

CHAPTER 6

WHAT TO CONSIDER DURING TRANSITIONING TO SCRUM

If you are contemplating transitioning to Scrum you need to know consider a few things before you get started. No matter the size of the organization, transitioning to Scrum is no easy task. So, here are three things to consider before diving in.

1.   Understand what you are getting into. For individuals who want to move the organization to Scrum and Agile but don't really understand what it means. This is a recipe for disaster. To describe Agile, let say it is a state of mind. But this state of mind is difficult for some, and while transitioning to Scrum is trendy, it is not a good reason to take your team through it. Ask yourself if you know what it means to be Agile. Can you adopt the Agile principles and values (Respect, Focus, Commit, Courage, and Openness)? Agile is a philosophy, one which believes code should be worked iteratively and incrementally, where business requirements are not written all up front. Would you be

willing to forgo BRD's? Would you be willing to empower your team?

2.   Still interested in transitioning to Scrum? Then you need to consider getting a Scrum coach. This individual will help you through the transition. They should ask you a lot of tough questions to help you get there. Outline your goals and walk them through it. Make sure your goals agree with the reason you choose to transition. If they don't, go back and review. The coach will help keep you in check and help teams keep these goals in mind. They will identify Scrum anti-patterns and give you suggestions on how to correct these patterns. They help grow your teams and look to keeping an Agile environment.

3.   Now that you have your Scrum coach, engage other departmental managers that are necessary for the success of your teams. Make an agreement with these other line managers up front that will cover approvals that may be required, changes in process that may need to be made. Have your Scrum Coach document this engagement model to communicate it to all involved. This is your first step in aligning the Business line to IT. Make it count! Show your commitment to addressing the business needs. Don't talk methodology; discuss how you plan on meeting their needs. You are seeking a partnership, so reach out as far as you need to. It will be worth every minute you spend.

HOW TO CHOOSE A SCRUM PILOT?

When an organization decides to implement the Scrum method of Agile software development, its first task is to determine which project will make the best pilot. Without previous experience in Scrum environments, selecting that initial project can seem like a guessing game. What makes one project better suited for success with Scrum than another anyway? Choosing projects isn't a science and those who have worked on numerous Scrum projects likely have an intuitive sense for which ones will take off and which ones will sink. However, there are a number of factors that affect the potential success of a project. Considering how these issues related to the business, the project in question, and the technology available will likely make an organization's decision-making process easier.

In terms of business considerations, the best Scrum pilots are those that demonstrate success for senior management. Impressing the value of the management paradigm upon an organization's leadership is critical for adoption, so it's important to choose a project that will impact the bottom line-and, consequently, have leadership's attention.

When examining a group of potential pilots, there are a number of questions that can be asked to determine how appropriate a project will be to demonstrate Scrum's efficiency.

1.   Does the project have a single, dedicated Product Owner? Working with an individual customer helps streamline communication and eliminate confusion among the team.

2.   Is there an experienced Scrum coach or mentor attached to the project? If yes, the team has an ally with a plethora of experience, from best practices to impediment resolution, to help steer the project toward success.

3.   Is the entire team working in a single location? While collocation is not a requisite for Scrum, it certainly simplifies things.

When a team works in a team room or in close proximity, Scrum's tenets of communication and collaboration can flourish. A geographically distributed team, on the other hand, typically requires a Scrum tooling solution to bring a team together.

4.   How well known are the project's requirements? One of the reasons Scrum works so well in software development is because it provides structure to the relative chaos of coding. This means that a project that has poorly defined requirements or no documentation would make a good choice for a pilot.

5. Is the team cross-functional? Scrum advocated cross-functional teams, so, if a project team is already composed of team members with the necessary range of skills, the team is that much closer to doing Scrum. The reasons for this are simple. When a team is capable of performing every stage of the development cycle, from analysis to testing, the feedback loop is shortened, thereby enabling a team to uncover problems - and address them - quickly.

The final consideration concerns the technological resources available to the team. Namely, does the team have the equipment and tools it needs to do its work? And what Agile programming practices are they employing during development? I would recommend using Continuous Integration, Test Driven Development, as well as Pair Programming, all of which tighten up processes and help Scrum teams perform to their potential.

If there's no single clear indication of a project's potential success with Scrum, there are still a number of factors that can help an organization narrow its options and make an informed selection.

SCRUM IMPEDIMENTS

In the Scrum method of Agile development, a scrum impediment is defined as anything that stands in the way of a team's productivity. This can literally be anything, from a team member who isn't pulling their weight to an uncomfortably warm team room. But if it's keeping the team from working at optimal efficiency, it's an impediment.

Luckily, Scrum dedicates an entire role to the resolution of these impediments: the ScrumMaster. The ScrumMaster works in a variety of capacities, such as helping the Product Owner prepare the backlog or radiating Scrum artifacts, but the primary responsibility of a ScrumMaster is to remove Scrum impediments and facilitate a high-performing team. To help the ScrumMaster achieve this, the team is responsible for communicating what barriers are impeding their progress. This occurs each day in the daily Scrum, when team members report on their accomplishments for the past 24 hours, goals for the next 24 hours, and what Scrum impediments stand in their way. This systematized feedback loop ensures that a Scrum Master always knows what is keeping the team from success and works to remove them.

Scrum impediments can apply to an organization's adoption of the Scrum method of agile software development, as well. Just as a broken keyboard, for example, would hinder a team member from coding, an attitude resistant to change (a "culture clash") bars a smooth Scrum adoption. In instances such as these, a company needs an organizational advocate to persuade management of the benefits of Scrum. In essence, that advocate is functioning as a Scrum Master by eliminating barriers to productivity even before a single Scrum team has been created. Of course, even an internal Scrum advocate does not ensure that a company will clearly see the potential of Scrum and migrate to agile practices. But, like the Scrum Master who works closely with a team to remove impediments, an internal Scrum advocate can help enact positive change and contribute toward an organization's success with Scrum.

SCRUM BACKLOG

In the Scrum method of agile software development, the single most important artifact is the product backlog. The product backlog is a list of all the requirements necessary for a system, project, or product. In essence, it is comprehensive to-do list, prioritized by the business value each piece of work will generate. But from a philosophical standpoint, the scrum backlog is what drives the business - by breaking down the big-picture story into manageable increments of work called Product Backlog Items (PBIs).

During the sprint planning meeting, the Scrum team negotiates with the Product Owner about what work they will take on during the next iteration. At this point, the Product Owner moves PBIs from the product backlog (basically, everything the company needs to do) into the sprint backlog, which is limited to the work to be completed in the next iteration.

So what does a product backlog look like? That depends on whether a Scrum team uses manual agile or an agile tool to monitor development progress. With manual agile, a team would create a list of its backlog items on a dry erase board, Post It notes, or a task board. This works great for teams who all work in the same office or room because every team member can easily consult the product backlog, the sprint backlog, and the status of its stories.

When Scrum teams are geographically dispersed, however, they often require a tool to help them manage their Agile software development. There are a number of tools on the market designed to bring un-collocated teams together with a virtual task board.

SCRUM CHECKLIST

Understanding the fundamentals of Scrum is a very simple thing to do. However, putting it into practice in the world of deadlines, strong characters and the need for quick decisions can often make it a huge challenge to get the job done using the Scrum rules. There are often situations where the rules are forgotten and put to one side, especially when they are most needed.

Here we have put together this simple checklist that anyone can use on a daily basis. It covers:

- Checklists for the fundamental tasks of every Scrum role

- An overview and recap of each scrum meeting (time-box)

- Checklists for the preparation, carrying-out, and goals of every scrum meeting

Using these checklists, you can be prepared and confident that you are carrying out the Scrum practices on your daily job, boosting the productivity of your scrum team and increasing return on investment for the business. One section of the checklist is below.

THE SCRUM MASTER CHECKLIST

- Update list of impediments from daily scrum, emails and another contact

- Follow up on impediments above

- Order any team equipment

- Write sprint report to stakeholders (once a sprint)

- Chase up any information holding up sprint backlog (e.g. third-party supplied artifacts)

- Make sure burndown and task board are visible in team room

- Arrange meetings and have chats to coach any new or needy team members, product owners or stakeholders

THE PRODUCT OWNER CHECKLIST

- Update backlog daily with any changes

- Prioritize backlog daily based on business value

- Meet stakeholders when needed to coordinate and capture requirements

- Liaise with team to clarify requirements and make trade-offs communicate release plan to stakeholders

THE DEVELOPMENT TEAM CHECKLIST

- Update task board with time remaining on tasks

- Report any impediments to Scrum Master

- Communicate with Product Owner before attempting and after completing a story

- Achieve daily targets

- Maintain team communication

- Keep solutions simple

- Focus on ship-ability (e.g. using practices such as pair programming, code review, continuous refactoring)

CHAPTER 7

WHY SCRUM WORKS

REASONS WHY THE SCRUM MASTER ROLE WORKS

1.   Dedicated bulldozer: Unlike other frameworks, the role focuses one person on removing obstacles. This means that the team can concentrate on getting the job done.

2.   Dedicated coach: The role gives one-person responsibility for coaching others. No one can "pass the buck" on this. Therefore, one person has the focus of helping all members of the organization to understand the framework.

3.   Impartiality: A Scrum Master can be as helpful to a team as a product owner; without picking sides. The only focus is on making sure the framework and project is successful. This can help solve problems and gain trust.

4.   Responsibility for the framework, not delivery: This is almost reverse psychology. The Scrum Master is only concerned with making sure the framework is carried out as

the Scrum rules say. Divorcing the responsibility for the framework from the responsibility to deliver means that they can concentrate on making sure that rules are followed, which in turn creates a well-oiled machine. If the Scrum Master's job is done and everyone in the Scrum team is performing their role, then the development team can deliver.

5. No single point of control that could fail: Since a Scrum Master does not control the team, the absence of one does not leave the team in disarray. The Scrum Master sets up a system that everyone can follow in their absence.

REASONS WHY THE PRODUCT OWNER ROLE WORKS

1. Time maximized for business return on investment: The product owner is not responsible for delivering the work or maintaining the process but simply for making priority calls and maintaining the requirements backlog. This allows a great deal of focus.

2. A dedicated source of requirements: There is no one else in the organization that needs to be consulted on a project's requirements. Senior stakeholder requirements flow through the product owner for a single point of contact.

3. One person responsible for changes in requirements: As the business picture changes only one person needs to capture the new requirements and update them.

4. Achieves the best compromise: Even senior stakeholders will need to trust their product owner with the final decision. This aligns the business and makes appropriate compromises for the good of the product.

5. Aligns the customer and team, daily: This role is the interface between the business and the team. Their presence at all the scrum meetings means that the team is always acting on the latest information.

REASONS WHY THE DEVELOPMENT TEAM ROLE WORKS

1. A group of dedicated experts: Explicitly calling the team out as expert's means that Scrum teams are assembled to solve problems on their own. This frees up other roles to focus on their own areas of expertise.

2. Flexible to business needs: Scrum teams adapt to a given situation in order to get a product increment built. Any decisions should be tied only to a business requirement. This, in turn, gives a business long- and short-term flexibility and reduces wasted effort in favor of the targeted effort.

3.   Lean and cost effective: The small size combined with a high degree of expertise means that things get done to a high degree of quality with minimal technical communication.

4.   Less management needed: Teams organize themselves. This means that everyone else can concentrate on their own role.

5.   Highly scalable when given the resource: Large teams can be separated and organized through regular meetings called scrum-of-scrums. The teams each have Scrum Masters to keep them coordinated. Caveat - when two or more teams work on the same code-base, the team will need to decide if this is feasible.

WHY IS AGILE SCRUM METHODOLOGY DEEMED AS THE BEST?

1.   Clients can track changes

Gone are the days when clients were least interested in the development process developers follow. Today time equals money, where they want to get things done in the best possible way and as quickly as possible. This technology provides them with a definite set of benefits where they can keep full control over the entire process. They can set a proper time frame within which the project needs to be delivered. They are allowed to make changes in the requirements and priorities anytime if they wish to do so. This increases customer's satisfaction.

2.   Gives fast return on investments

Agile is the best trick to achieve faster returns on investments. This methodology is not just helpful for working for clients, but also for your own products. You can develop a product across iterations and can keep adding more features to it. This can give an extra edge to an organization, where they can launch a product with limited features and keep on adding the premium features afterward.

3.   Keeps the risk levels low

Regular feedback from prospective clients is a great way to reduce market risk. Getting timely feedback from prospect clients can assist in making the product better and reduce the risk of not meeting their expectations. The project is easily accessible to the clients during its life cycle. Even if the client wants to make a cancellation in the early stages, you can easily handle that. Thus, it imparts better accessibility and visibility to clients in order to make correct decisions.

4.   Better management process

Agile Scrum methodology leverages certain benefits to the management team in an organization. As the entire developmental process is pretty much predictable, there is a good chance for better workforce management. The relationship between clients and team members also gets better, which creates better future prospects.

5.   Enhanced product quality

Agile methodologies generally result in best quality products. When the experts and clients are in constant contact, clients can always ask experts about the best possible technology that can be followed. Cross-functional development teams including developers, testers, programmers, analysts, and writers work together as a single team. Their collaborative efforts will automatically result in the best quality and reliable product.

CHAPTER 8

SCRUM USER STORIES

In the Scrum method of agile software development, user stories are how work is expressed in the backlog. How a team decides to write its user stories is a matter of preference, but the user story must always be written from the perspective of the end user.

That is, team members are encouraged to conceive of their work from the standpoint of the consumer who will use it. A team might articulate a story as a noun or, more specifically, a feature to be built into a product, such as "text message" on a cell phone project or "speedometer" for an automobile manufacturer. Or the story could be stated in a sentence or phrase, such as "debug GPS tracking system."

Many Scrum teams have adopted Mike Cohn's user story template, in which a single sentence identifies who the end user is, what the end user wants, and why. This model of a user story is typically written like this: "As a [end user role], I want [the desire] so that [the rationale].

By way of illustration without placeholders, consider how a user story for a developer working on a calculator application for a PC might express the work. First, they would need to know who he is coding the application for a PC user. Secondly, they would want to determine what the PC user would want to use the application for: to have a convenient prepackaged calculator application. Finally, they would want to state why it's important that the PC user have this application. This is perhaps the least clearly defined piece of information, but one can assume that the developer might state the rationale would be to add, subtract, multiply, and divide-or to simply add value to the product. Thus, the final user story might read something like this: "As a PC user, I want a calculator with basic functionality on my PC so that I can conveniently perform basic mathematic operations and enhance my overall experience."

User stories are a way to document requirements from the perspective of the end user. Although stories can be written in a number of ways, Mike Cohn's model is of particular value for Scrum development teams because it provides the most information about the story, including for whom it is being built and why. By orienting the story to reflect the desires of the end user, user stories help developers remain focused on what the customer wants.

CONCLUSION

Scrum is an incremental framework around which to base agile project management, which can work really effectively in a wide range of projects. Sounds great right? But are you really ready to adopt Scrum methodologies? Plenty of our colleagues, peers, and friends have jumped right onto the Scrum bandwagon, enticed by the simplicity of it, without actually knowing if they are ready to add it to their projects.

They are tempted by short work cycles which produce functional software and the suggested ability to control and produce cycles of work simply by having daily meetings, and who wouldn't be? So, we get a certified Scrum master in place, get everyone behind the process, and make sure they understand it, and head into the Scrum sunset thinking how rosy everything will be.

But needless to say, this is not always the case. What many of those adopting Scrum don't always see it that the software engineering needs to be as ready for Scrum as the humans involved. Otherwise, after a few really successful sprints using Scrum, you will often hit a wall, where your productivity dips meaning software release dates are missed and customers get angry. This is when you decided that actually, Scrum isn't that great after all.

This situation usually arises when Scrum is adopted without the addition of other technical practices like Continuous Integration or Test Driven Development, as without these Scrum allows a team to work faster but often to the detriment of quality. So, in reality, the underlying problem isn't that Scrum as a project management tool doesn't work, but rather that Scrum doesn't (and possibly shouldn't) address the actual building of the software or its quality.

So, the fact of the matter is that however well you adopt Scrum, it is irrelevant if the engineering of your software is not up to fulfilling the project's needs.

www.ingramcontent.com/pod-product-compliance
Lightning Source LLC
Chambersburg PA
CBHW070854070326
40690CB00009B/1833